Signals from the Other

Jennie Osborne

Signals from the Other

First Edition 2022

Jennie Osborne has asserted her authorship and given permission to
Dempsey & Windle for these poems to be published here.

Published by Dempsey & Windle under their VOLE imprint

15 Rosetrees
Guildford
Surrey
GU1 2HS
UK
01483 571164
dempseyandwindle.com

A catalogue record for this book is available from the British Library

British Library Cataloguing-in-Publication Data

ISBN: 978-1-913329-74-7

Printed and bound in the UK

SIGNALS FROM THE OTHER

Many people have contributed to this journey in many ways – those who have shared their knowledge of nature, or walks on the moor, the artists with whom I have collaborated, the poets who have given valuable feedback, and especially Steve Day and Julie-ann Rowell, who each played a part in helping me shape this collection. My thanks to them, and also to Sophia Roberts whose beautiful textile work has given me the cover.

Many thanks also to the following artists whose work provided starting points for some of the poems in this book:
Ann Chester-King (*Predator*); Andy Coldrey (*And There Were No Boundaries*); Rosemary Ensor (*Volcanic*); Josie Gould (*A Morrigan For Our Time, Gaia No Longer Remembers Herself*); Christine Linfield (*Otter Of Land And Water*); Bev Samler (*Hindsight, Blaze*).

Jennie Osborne

for Steve
for everything

Acknowledgements

Some of these poems have previously been published:

'Concerning'	*The North*, Aug 2019
'The Smallest Monkey in the World'	*The Broadsheet*, Aug 2017 *Counting Down the Days,* Grey Hen, 2021
'Caer Bran'	*Further Than It Looks* Grey Hen 2019
'Crow Place'	*Poets, Painters and* *Printmakers,* Bulb Store Books 2012
'And The Wolf'	*The High Window* Summer 2021

'Fossils' was commended in the *Troubadour Poetry Competition,* 2016

Contents

CONCERNING

Concerning my garden, it is a bastion of bramble.
Concerning bramble, it is threaded by couch-grass.
Concerning couch-grass, it runs sly as rumour.
Concerning rumour, it travels by satellite and mouths.
Concerning mouths, they thirst and blister.
Concerning blisters, they are coin-sized weapons.
Concerning weapons, they are tools in the game.
Concerning games, there's the business of keeping score.
Concerning scores, they are measured in bodies.
Concerning bodies, they bleed and they burn.
Concerning burning, it brings char and purging.
Concerning purging, read gardens, bodies, scores.

ELEPHANTS UNPLUGGED

Because they were plugged into acacia trees
that grew on the site of the airport
and the transcontinental highway

Because they were plugged into watercourses
that no longer trickle from the Nile

Because they were plugged into their matriarch
who was felled by poachers
for her tusks

Because their mourning haunted
your television and spoilt your evening

you switched them off
pulled out the plug.

THE FALKLANDS WOLF

They came to meet us, tails raised,
curious overgrown pups, mongrels
of fox, wolf, dingo, massive as mastiffs,
bounding towards us, meeting our signature
on the South Atlantic gusts, white tail tips twitching.

Like some garbled nightmare, after a journey
through tropics, toyed with by waves
like roiling walls, driven by wind to weather
more familiar, this spatter of rocks more Scottish Isles
than South Sea atolls.

Penguins were easy picking, seemed
the only sizeable creatures on the island
other than sea-slipping seals, and their meat
welcome after hard-tack months. Then came the pack
like a parody of faithful hounds.

The seabirds scattered. Ship's mate
stood his ground, reached out his hands
to the lolling tongues, the fishy breath.
In one, a scrap of penguin.
In the other, a knife.

*The 'Falklands Wolf' was a distinct class of canid which diverged from its
nearest relatives 7 million years ago. They were first discovered by sailors
in 1690, and the last was killed in 1876, 40 years after being described by
Charles Darwin.*

SIGNALS FROM THE OTHER

It's a game that's gone on for millennia
between those with an ear fit to listen
and that with a multitude of names
which speaks with more than tongues
has blown its whistle more loudly each decade.

Some find they need to put their heads
to the ground to catch the litany of mole rats
or the rattle of gods. Some swear
by dreams but their dictionaries disagree –
a case of pick and mix at the new age bazaar.

Some follow the tracks of tiger or vole
as they peter off towards extinction,
or interpret the bees' last messages,
the kakapo's failing language, witness
the redwood's blazing groans.

These days, it's more a matter
of shedding earmuffs, ripping off blinkers,
turning down the *eat me, buy me* white noise
and peeling off the plastic gloves, putting
an ear or a fingertip to any throbbing pulse.

And what we choose to be deaf to
has given up on subtle, given up on
the liquid language in lost eyes, diminishing
chords spring after spring, starved soil's
crunch as it turns to sand.

Seas have tried tantrum, rivers given lessons
in weeping. Every day the assemblage of ghosts
thickens, their silent accusation nudging through the ether,
tapping out its Mayday in minds which have cracked
the carapace, dare to be naked to our own complicity.

It's time for stormy crescendo, turning up
the heat, for waves of howl so strong
they lift us, hurl us, shatter us, drown us,
leave us to lie among oil-smothered fish, poisoned
cetaceans on a plastic-studded beach

and soon there will be unmaking, the first
threads are pulled. We can't say
there was no signal.

THIRTEEN WAYS
OF LOOKING AT AN UNIDENTIFIED BIRD

She scuttles through the garden
scattering a camouflage of leaves
Has this bird been told
she can't fly?

I call her she.
I don't know
if she is a he
or something else.
Neither does s/he.

Her feathers are splattered
by genetics.
With white paint
or bird shit? Maybe
she knows which.

Her beak is unremarkable
and nevertheless effective.
It concerns itself with tiny matters
among the leaf litter.

Although the size
and habit of a blackbird
she has taken a vow
of silence.

Crows inhabit
the tall beech
noisy in their pronouncements.
The unidentified bird
keeps her head down.

She won't tell me
where she has come from
even when geese fly over
calling the restless to follow.
She won't tell
the sparrows either.

Some days I think I love
an overgrown corner
by the pond
where a medium-sized bird
hangs out.
Other days I'm not
so sure.

A redpoll called in
to drink at the pond.
The unidentified bird
was unimpressed.

She does not hold
with bonfires unless
they are for burning
pictures of neat
symmetrical birds.

The bird believes
there may be
another of her kind.
She has no evidence
of this unless
she sees it in the pond.

A woman and an unidentified bird
are mismatched fractions.

A woman who pretends
to be a wild goose
or a nightingale
is in fact an unidentified bird
with random markings
who scurries from one side
of the garden
to the other.

THAT GOOD SLEEP

Given the choice
        I would be dormouse
                or anything small
                        that hibernates
                                has no power
                                        to mar the world

Even though I know
        the diggers are coming
                the oak that this blind follower of instinct
                        has chosen for its long sleep
                                is earmarked
                                        for felling

Even though I know
        the waters are rising
                the wood that bounds its world
                        will be
                                in weeks
                                        a swamp

I would go gladly
        into that good sleep
                curled in my temporary haven
                        my parcel nest of bark
                                among the roots
                                        wrapped in myself

letting the before slip off
        like moult
                guarding no nut called spring
                        in my imaginings
                                no hope it might sprout
                                        unblighted

STAG

The year is a clearing
where a stag leaps in

tramples ferns and saplings
that thought they were important

throws back his head
shows the pale vulnerability
of his throat.

It's not the antlers that impress
it's that tender curve.

I can see it
berried red.

THE SMALLEST MONKEY IN THE WORLD

clings on by its tail to the last tree
in the Brazilian rainforest,
looks me in the eye, full of questions,
knows me as family, if from a distant branch.

A miniature hand, like that
of an infant's infant grasps my finger
although this new acquaintance
could sit in my child-sized palm.

We have them in our fist, these small
relations, each family, each tribe,
their home, their neighbourhood, the extent
of their known world all in our grasp

and we are squeezing as we chop away
at the trunk of the family tree.

MURMURATION

sooting the horizon, a tinnitus of sky, a space between storms. The crows wait in their wings' black cloaks. I have borrowed my feathers from the jay but not her habit of raiding nests. I meet you here, under a sky churning with potential, amazed at your strength, a standing stone weathered by weather. What happens in the space between us? Electricity of a living storm, suspended within cloud. We have been scattered to four winds like bones picked over, dropped by crows, like birds in mutable formation rearranged by storm, and still we stand, the space between us live, thrumming with murmuration.

CAER BRAN

                Sky

              the wide bowl
and being up in it   in the scoured air
              out of the moist woods

Green wears camouflage colours
dun   sage   pewter   beige
bush and stone sharing a palette

Gorse and bracken clump   push in
            on squeezed paths

What remains of rampart
    is still on guard

White butterfly wearing a trellis of grey
settles on a slab   moves on

        This is wind's country
never off duty   it chases lassitude
        back down the contour
            to the valleys

        You are waiting for me
at home here in this high place
        of the protector

All horizon   land falling away
        until it topples into haze
beyond is what we have left behind

We walk the rim   sound the bowl of sky.

DISPATCHES

There are maps through this country
so we're told   but I'm
not finding them
in the open mouths between lyrics
or the uncut pages
of a book too costly to open

so I'm cobbling my own
from grounded leaves   rumours of dust-clouds
scratchings I scribble
on paper creased and stained
with moorland
seeped through from another journey

a journalist of the soul   not knowing
what words to wear or whether
it's the temple bells I follow
or the last blackbird

and now we're drawn into
another moody winter
banking food as though we know
it will be the last currency

wish we had listened
to words our mothers   spoke without owning
handed down from ancestors
with maps etched in their bones

In order not to surrender
we sit in streets   where earth
is straitjacketed in concrete
listen for footpaths   creeping
up through cracks
long for our own tiny Edens

I make smudged and crossed-out charts
in case there will be anyone to follow
or some accident of time or space
we might call
destination

SHORTEST DAY UP STONETOR

she's in disguise   pretty as Christmas
as a sugared cake
not liking this party-dress
nubbled underneath   chilled
to marrow   all her veins frozen

mauled by footsteps
not wanting   this trampling
hard shouldered   bruising back
springy pelt brittled
wire-sharp and biting

holding her traps   beneath her skirts
trip-wires set and waiting
to bring down
any unbelonging

she's not playing today
she means it

SHE WONDERS HOW A WOLF MAKES A CHOICE

She reads about wolves
how a pack has rules
hierarchy of scent
no place for divergence
no possibility of lies

how some choose to leave
or find that choice made for them
one track of paws across the snow
hunting small
no patch to call territory
howl answered by its echo

she tries but fails
to strip away human
that knitting of stories
or weighing of consequences
get down to what it is
flicks like a signal
in blood, brain, muscle

prompts this turning
with low-slung tail
pack shed like last year's pelt
as she follows her nose
strange messages on the air
fresh trails to lay down

one open door
one track of feet across the snow

SALTMARSH

When river gets within a breath
   of sea   where thrust of current matches
         push of tide   where silt has settled
tough pioneers   glasswort and cordgrass
   set up camp   are joined
by other species that live on the edge
         sea lavender   sea aster   thrift

Not a place for the unwary
   they step here at their risk
criss-crossed with creeks   studded
   with island tussocks   haunted with left behind
voices of departed geese   a muted landscape
         caught in shades of dawn   before the sun's
   got up and raised a smile

Best to have wings   for aerial scan
   of salt pan and scrape   for the quick getaway
         made for transients this patch   butterflies
in October   the lazy lapwing flocks
         no place for maps   the marsh rewrites itself
   with every season   every wash of tide
nothing stays long   banks shift   the river rises   year
   on year   this is a place in transit
         going   gone

FIFTY MILLION TREES

Fifty million trees, they say,
will write the gospel of creation,
a knotty business, not for novices,
a weighing up of soil and tenant species,
selecting those in need
of somewhere to put down roots
among the roots, deep under,
where mycellium plait the threads
of their bush telegraph testament.

Great oaks may come from acorns
but their nursery needs midwives,
those sent to prepare the way,
the birches, willows, hawthorns
mulching the cradle, knitting a canopy.
No cookie-cutter woodland but a quilt
of grove and glade and copse and clump.

Their days are written in centuries,
but now the need for fast forward,
for acceleration of profusion, turns
human parasite, the villain of the piece
into reluctant ally on the only road
to redemption. No time for random,
for a one-in-twenty chance of coming
through, this caravan needs all as crew
to reach the next millennium.

Beavers and bees, dung-rolling beetles,
each blindly stitching its seam – and some
will fall and leave their own-shaped hole
to be patched as best another species can,
or gape. The weave will shift and skew.
We dig, we carry water laced with guilt
and try to kid ourselves it is not leaking.

OTTER OF LAND AND WATER

She brings the river
    with her its spume
        and rapids as she
            rises

She brings the earth
    with her its ores
        and quartz into
            air

She has a story
    to tell of the
        moor beneath
            pretty

She is smeared with sediment
    tail hinting at eel
        forepaws suggesting
            fins

She searches for scents
    rumours of storm
        eyes peat-dark
            pools

REMNANT

above its mossed canopy
      antennae bristle with seed-direction
         but receive no signal

a rainforest in miniature
      crumbles at a touch
         a spillage of dry-air plankton

both scent and moisture have deserted
      while I look away
         more grains lose hold

its voice is neither whisper
      nor the echo of whisper
         but paper's memory

         of sibilant unstitching

REBELLION

These dandelions – no show girls
but they know how to pop up
where they're not wanted
go on, do your worst
on tarmac and paving stone
Parliament Square, Waterloo Bridge
padlocked into earth with combination roots
go on, arrest me
not ashamed to flaunt
the green rosette around their petals
rewilding the conurbation
raising the question of offence
with ranks of blue lawnmowers
doing their job, keeping order.

And in the borders, doing what they do
and in orchards and gardens beyond,
the healing herbs, berry bushes,
apple and peartrees sending their fruit –
in every open space, every town centre
they're flowering in solidarity
clematis clinging on, geraniums
making a statement, even
under the hedges, a host
of violets quietly clicking send.

WHAT'S WRONG WITH SPRING?

Back in the dark time
I held to spring like a lifebelt
each primrose   each snowdrop
a necessary message from the future
that I would come through
life begin again

What could be wrong with spring?

birds that haven't made it back
from winter journeys   lost in the Sahara
shot down over Italy

shrinking woodlands   fields going down
under armies of houses

warnings of choking dust
breath laced with poison

looking at Devon hedgebanks
in yellow and white for Easter
seeing rubble   craters
charred crops   scorched trees
one country after another
war their only season

knowing for some birds
some fields   some people
some nations
spring will not come
this year or next

POWER PLAY ON THE COASTAL LINE

This was the Everest of waves
a titan teenager bursting with tantrum
biting at the rich red cake of cliff
snatching at bushes, fences
snapping signal poles like matches
picking up train and track and throwing them
into the air and out of the game.

We'd wait it out, we said,
retreat to what surely must be
safe distance, gather what random toys
it had hurled back at us
thankful we still had electric power.

Maybe the water-brat had views on power –
what we'd done when we had
the chance – brewed up a righteous rage.
Maybe the storm-hiss was its laughter
as it put us in our place.

I'll show you power. It did. Then
as we started to pick up, put back,
we found it had invited all its friends.

YOU'VE BEEN THIS WAY BEFORE

Nothing at rest here, only
a river headlong, not caring
what's stirred up
fingled from rocks and silt
from all the cracked goodbyes
the prayers and curses
dropped over this bridge.

Beeches are seasoned bystanders
their leaves quaking.
They know what's coming.

If you wanted peace
this wasn't the place to come.

Clouds shoulder in
pushing straggles of blue
out of the way, faster
than you believed possible.

You've been here before.
You know what happens

how lightning sparks those colours –
yes, those, the dangerous ones –
from unassuming surfaces

what storm can do with branch and boulder
with water – especially with water.

Don't play the innocent.
The trees knew what was coming
as soon as you stepped
onto the bridge.

FLIPPER

is what they call him
the land ones who find fish in air
swim clumsily with the smell of fear
in this spoilt water

He does not know this as name
knows only the sound his mother made
through the living water
when she spoke him

He still tries to speak her
but this place
is an echo with no answers

He swims round and round
through the tight days
dead fish   dead water
shouts like hunting
from the fish-throwers

Once there was a female
not his mother
she smelt of wrong-body   of tired
she sank to the bottom
stopped seeking air

He wants to stay at the bottom
not to surface into sharp light
sounds that hurt his cavities
to let his lungs fill
with the killed water

He tries but something in him drags him up

When he leaps, he sees
                        an echo of himself
in the wall of solid air

One day he takes his largest leap
into echo   into stopping

            head   thrust forward

            raised
      flipper
one

ONCE WE WERE FORESTS

taller than eyes can reach

companies of cousins
in slowest motion

grasping under soil each others' roots
passing our underground morse

lifting our heads to salute the sun
shaking limbs in answer to wind

and we were communities
our bodies insect highways

our crooks and canopies bird nurseries
each lulled with its own drone or serenade

we were glad with their song

and we were colour symphonies
wore arpeggios of green

flaunted open-mouthed trumpets tubas piccolos
in every rainbow shade

and we were one in many   many in one

look at the sand
      see where a tide has left our image in sepia relief

water remembers   leaves this monoprint
      pale ghost of what is lost

listen as it repeats our song
      wind in leaves
               leaves
                  leaves

PLASTIC FISH

I wonder if it still has patient gills
filtering what it needs to live,
whether it's given up on mouthparts,
takes in what sustenance
this ocean soup offers through its skin,
converts each molecule to backbone, fin,
plast-organic brain.

LOVE LIES LARGELY WHERE YOU FIND IT
(after Gary Rosenthal)

and it is what a tree does
      lifting its face to the sun
          having invented solar panels

and it is what a tree does
      puffing out warning to its neighbours
          of beetle attack   aphid attack

and it is what a tree does
      pumping sugar to its dying neighbour
          root to root

and it is what a bird does
      scavenging in snow-bare patches
          to fill insistent gapes

and it is what I do
      stacking logs   stoking the hearth
          to comfort the chased and injured thing
             that curls there shivering

CLOSE TO THE WIND

Young, and not yet grown
into the way of hawk,
three gapes open in not-knowing,
blood-instinct under their tongues,
their yellow claw-fingers grasp air,
itch for rabbit-neck.

They have been named in the old language,
as if that charm would keep them
through all odds,
named Ghost, Light, Sky,
to breathe height into their wings,
been braceleted with numbers
to count the days of their passage,
the days of their deaths.

And they will be launched forth,
pushed into air as seal into water,
into unarmoured air that offers
no refuge, into the sights
of shotguns

the harriers harried, brought low
with lead, leaving their plotted tracks
to those who collect knowledge

no legacy to their own kind,
thrust in their turn
into the spring breeze on the Carneddau,
none except an impression
of tail feather dipping into cloud,
an almost-call at the edge of hearing,

awyr   golau   ysbryd
sky   light   ghost.

PREDATOR

sky is a spilt page
    up here where we
        used to have footing
all the edges
    blurring smudging
        leaked on   although
            the year has been so dry
and fields are swimming
    tall things standing
        are not trees
            true name not to be seen
nothing of bird
    except falling
        except knots of feather
            caught in low thorns
still something hovers
    leaving its shadow
        vast
like no predator seen before

VOLCANIC

Maybe it started with a pebble –
a glance I mean   a word or two
a foot straying the wrong side
of an unmarked boundary

However it began   it grew
its own momentum –
was it a kiss   a rumour on social media
a storm gathering its resentment

Now we're all caught up
in rush and thrust
ground we thought firm under our soles
backslid to boulders
smashing at anything solid

We fight to keep our vehicle
on the road   lose purchase
on tracks crumbling to edge

each of us plucked up
whirled and flung
like any lump of rock

From deep inside   fire forces
its way out
chars yesterday
brands tomorrow
as its own

SOAKAWAY

Under dug earth
next to the cats' graves
a chamber holds the hills' weeping

a stopped place
swelled with flow
longing for the stream

pent under pressure
water broods
grows sour

spends itself
in hard clay soil
one tear at a time

SAUNTON SANDS

beach coming back   recovering from invisible

from indoors   from dodging backs   from turning faces

beach is lifting its many heads

to burn   in dreamed-of sun

in clumps around blankets   coolbags   windbreaks

distanced by guesstimetres

its tides rushing out

along   stretched   wet   sands

to meet the mirror surge

of waves

then ebbing back

and in

an aerial sign of disapproval

for this break of quarantine

enter   black frowned clouds

to the sound of shelling

in the sky

a fusillade of rain

      that builds and builds

          bombards

             sends the beach

like a panicked nest of ants

      burrowing under canopies

gathering sodden   scrambling back

      into the box

HINDSIGHT

And we look up
those of us left
up at this carboned remnant
this linocut
of what we knew as green

and there are sands between us
and the world we loved
oil-smeared   already slipped
through the hour-glass
a one-way travel.

From this black hump in time
the line is clear
as though cut with a knife
between now and before
and ours the hands behind the blade

but then it seemed smudge
a collage of good intentions
we didn't put our weight behind
while we could.

Those black memorials stood as trees
those cracks sang clear in stream.

For a little longer
we will remember green.

PLANET

Rocking from north to south,
bombed off its axis,
wormholed into pumice,
forcefed poison,
spitting, scratching, slapping back
at its own parasite,
hit-and-run wind, grumbling rock,
tiny mutation
of tiny virus
after tiny virus.

INKLING

Not so much a premonition
as a postcard from the post-syntactical
a tweet from the post-cyber.

Nothing in words, those having atrophied
back to breath, no –
it made use of the ephemeral,

specks that might have been petals
in a floraceous era, caught in the firemesh
of a starless night.

We'd lost the art of augury
together with speaking in tongues, oneiromancy.
We'd been through the digital, the sub-etheric.

Quantum had dissolved the time illusion.
We'd numbed the visceral energy every which way,
chemical, electronic, transcendental.

Exactly how the message could be received
was uncertain, but somehow it got through.
Meticulously, uniformly, we prepared for departure,

just as though there was anywhere
left to go.

SKIN QUESTIONS

Do you spend your nights
casting silver bullets in your forge
ready for the day
I turn up at the door?

Did you see me once
slipping into my other skin?
Was that why you stopped looking
avoided my nakedness?

Why do I have the feeling
the body you fear is
no pent bundle of claw and fur
but woman's flesh?

What would I find if I looked
in the wardrobe you keep so well locked?

A MORRIGAN FOR OUR TIMES

It's about standing with a foot in each continent
pulsing garnet, the old year's blood, extending
broken spokes of fingers, stretching
to hold the tired fabric together

knowing she can only fail
and all that matters
this standing firm, this failing
this standing, still
as the soil under her soles
crumbles into mad-eyed ocean

GAIA NO LONGER REMEMBERS HERSELF

She has left her face behind
shawled herself in fuchsia, rose
shades the last dawn left behind

in memory of flowers

She is down to her bones now
cracking their lengths into gravel

Her empty eye-pits film with plastic

Once   she breathed the seas
beat with their push   their pull

Now breath is clot and stoppered
her every surface slimed
with unliving

She can't remember light
the dance of photosynthesis and transpiration

Almost   she has gone under

GRANDDAUGHTER

You won't be reading this.
Not even in that particular multiverse
where I missed a pill and birthed your mother.
But I conjure you up, small and quick,
(genes tell), a curious eye, a quirk
about the mouth that says you don't give up
too easily.
              And what I want to say
is sorry, for how I let them all slip through
my fingers, those fellow-travellers I failed
to keep secure. You might have seen them
on your screens, along with basilisks
and unicorns.
              Words, too, let me down.
How can I describe the singing ecosphere
that is a whale? Or ask you to imagine
your pet cat (you'll have one if you can, I'm sure)
but pony-sized, each striped
with its own name, untamed as the jungle
it used to patrol. Maybe on your earth
there will be jungle left.
                          I'd like to paint for you
more stripes, a smaller scale this time, those buzzing
engines of pollination we called bees.
                          Whatever's left you,
cherish it. Spend your whole life to save the smallest ant.
I'm glad you won't be here, on this trashed world
to sweat as it heats up, as friendly air runs out.

DRIFTLINE

My toes snag on fishing net,
one of those vast trawls, straggled across the width of a cove,
waves champing at it, drowning it then running away,
their thrash, thrash, thrash
making its point again, again, again
on the sucked sand.

The day is washed in blues infiltrated by grey,
blues that have had their hearts broken,
cracked hearts in return.

No gulls to be heard, no shearwaters
or cormorants. In my head, their complaint reverberates.

It might be late afternoon.
Whatever time it is, is running out.

Around the headland, a faded sign on a wire-mesh fence
bears a yellow symbol, reads DANGER
RADIOACTIVE   KEEP OUT.

Caught up in the net at my feet
one rag of oil-dark wing. I count the years
since we tried to clean them, tried
to stretch a safety net, halt
the encroaching tide.

FOSSILS

A morning scumbled in grey
    layer
      slab
        pavement

        all the ancient creatures
tombed   underfoot

      in flakes
falling out of the marvellous
      layer-cake cliff
sepia   honey ash

mist made solid
        at the point of crumble

and we
    walking through tilt

sky at brim
        of dissolving
            of indecision
    mumbling us
clammy finger stroking us

water   keeping its distance
      biding

    although we know about tides

its slugtrail slime
          unfooting us
on innocent surfaces

no distance   nothing round

the headland except
                               nuclear no-go zone
we choose
            not to imagine

looking for colours at our feet

            rock flaking under

no lines intact
        landscape
            reinventing
practising   (are we?)

        for what comes next

AND THERE WERE NO BOUNDARIES

This is us
   when we were trackless
on the cold moor

   dreaming the gone time   the not yet time
when you were branch   and I was twig
   when you were wall   and I was stile

this is us
   danced out of our shapes
        into detour
into leat and runnel
   into sheeptrack and gorse

twisted to hidden and out-of-sight
   to slippage and mire
        to flounder and divergence

your roots are loosing from soil
   my hands are nothing but lines on a map

I am bird becoming wing
   searching for your barked and rippled trunk

but there is tor and gorge between us
   sky clouds us in
        and all is white

DISPLACED

this sparrow   blown off course
    uplifted   dropped
into hubble of hubbub

bustled by hustle
trollied and clanged
tangled in jangle

                within an arch of chant

talked over in jumbled syllable
        in scratchy sound
           in slicety knives

this sparrow   small in the size of it
                the city of it
                   the moving parts of it

in the growl and fume of it
    buffet and drag of it

peril of underwheel   of crush
    of thudfoot   of boot   of grind

                within an arch of chant

no eyes ears heart   for a handful of feather
    a dumbed tongue   drowned
in cacoph cacoph cacopho...

        alarm!   alarm!

            an arch of chant is not a place of safety

CROW PLACE

Blackness

wing canopies covering   keeping a lid

glints sharp as nighteyes   sharp as beaks

no fairy-come-follow goldie yammer

We feather-leaf here   incubate

we burrow-root sett here   cubsuckle

Nestraiding loudfoot   thief kill-scent

we tooth against   we claw we

root   hole   tangle   thorn

we nettlebite   stonebreak   soilsmother

Strange enternest   we hatch into earth

rootfood   wormfood

all brood   all blackness make

CONSERVATION

Opening the window
my hands showered
with half-unravelled knots

    husks of what was fly
    last summer
    miniature body-parts
              disassembling
    on the windowsill

and here and there
among the spatter

        one on its back
        feebly thrashing

knowing it futile
      I took time
           uprighted
                the friable bodies

released the catch
launched them on one last flight.

KINDLING

It's about finding a point of ignition
on a stave drawn at the foot of the balance sheet,
weighing chalice against stanza,
epiphany against arpeggio.
Follow the enjambement from vestment
to villanelle. Take an interest
in the counterpoint of shoreline, or horizon
and any of the above. It will spark
if you feed in enough
of any kind of capital.
Maybe not in the chapel,
the library, the concert hall,
maybe in the compost heap
or in the piss-painted alley
behind the kebab bar and the betting shop.
It's about listening to everything
you don't want to hear.

THE BIRDS OF VALENCIA

First it was the goldfinch,
swinging in its cage on the sandstone balcony
in the Carrer Major, calling to its flock,
live flowers flitting up and down the ravine.

      All night the caged birds call her name.

Then a parakeet, the yellow of celandines,
in a meshed enclosure on a first-floor terrace,
embroidering its song with wolf-whistles, church bells,
displaying to his own reflection.

      All night the caged birds peck at her thoughts.

And then a partridge from a high-walled yard,
her cry a chord of desire and loneliness
luring her suitors from the dry terraces
to face the loud lust of guns.

      All night the caged birds claw
      at net and chicken-wire,
      chirp of ladders, wire-cutters, keys

      of the hour between three and four
      when owls rule and nightingales in the lemon trees
      mourn the prisoners.

      All night the caged birds scream.

NIGHT WATCHING

Tonight the clock crawls, edging
along the brink of night, reluctant
to leave this tattered year behind
all its unfinished business
trailing behind it like a kid's coat
through the gutter.

This is not about reason. Nothing
here is reasonable now. The day
was full of laughs and kisses
and the year ahead waves at us
round the corner of the week
promising all we never dared
to dream, a personal paradise
that defies the times we live in.

But still, tonight, I listen
to the crackled grain of air
that fills the place of sleep
and watch you shift, uneasy
beside me, wanting
to haul me down to where
you float in that safe, needed
oblivion.

BLAZE

It's catching on
like worldwide wildfire

breathing the trees blue   then black
with dioxide breath

They're all doing it now

Siberia putting the heat   on its tundra

rainforest dried out
and crackling

This moor's had it inflicted
year on year
patch by careful patch

but now it's learning
what happens when sun meets glass
how a spark makes the most of itself
how brushwood is a co-conspirator
gorse and bracken flaring up

No good looking to the trees
they're collateral damage
clumping together
semaphoring branches
won't save them

Why take the slow track to extinction

when you can go
in a blaze?

PSALM

after John Coltrane 'A Love Supreme'

We mouth them on repeat until
they're full and empty as mantras,
our *Please God* and our *Alleluia*,
I love you and *Why me?*
The worn-out currency of words
stretched beyond their definitions
by volcanos which possess us,
burst out in uttered lava
that grows cold on blistered lips.

We sang before we spoke,
and some rare souls find deeper language,
first offspring of the primal cry.
Tonight, it's Coltrane's saxophone
that tells it how it is, how life
goes on under the bruises –
then reaches for the sky to seek
one last and everlasting listener.
Over the rolling grumble
of the world's drums, it speaks me.

AND THE WOLF
after Kim Moore 'And the Soul'

And the wolf
if she is to know herself
must sense into synapse and sinew,

limbs and skin,
find what manner of beast
she is hiding in

learn her pack, and the rules of her pack,
just which lines she must scent
smothered under snow

exactly how her hide
will be torn from her body
for a paw out of place

the precise degree of cower,
when to roll over and submit,
offering her belly to their teeth.

She must learn her howl,
practise it in silence
not to lose it in the chorus

be ready for the night
she takes her own track
into the wilderness of her self.

HOW IT WILL BE

This is how it will be
  after scrabble and grab
    after beg and dwindle
      after pox and puke

      these hollowed streets
      half-shadowed with haunts
      these house-shells clustered
      glowing with empty
      the hole across the bay
      they called Hinckley

This is how it will be
  after fire and flood
    after parch and mildew
      after starve and stab

      these scaffold trees
      crumbling to char
      these clots of fur and feather
      fences leaning slant
      still guarding bones
      and empty sockets

This is how it will be
    after babble and bleed
      after greed and grime
        after the pennies drop

this demented sun
smearing the tired gasp
of a smothered sea
which heaves its plastic trawl
this deafened air
this deafened air

This is how it will be...

Jennie Osborne

Jennie Osborne lives in South Devon. She is the Stanza Rep for Poetry Teignmouth and one of the Teignmouth Poetry Festival organisers. She is an occasional Poetry School tutor and ran many workshops in the area until Covid intervened. An active member of Dartmoor-based Moor Poets, she has edited two of their popular anthologies as well as appearing in them all.

Since the 1990s, her work has been published in numerous magazines and journals and she has won the Kent and Sussex Poetry Prize as well as the Ware Sonnet Prize and has been placed or commended in a number of other competitions. She has two previous collections, *How To Be Naked* and *Colouring Outside the Lines,* both from Oversteps Books.

Much of her work has involved collaboration with visual artists and musicians, and in 2022 she has a series of events planned with jazz and improvising musicians, including working as special guest with the Day Evans Dale Ensemble, live and on a recording for the Discus record label.